ACKNOWLEDGMENTS

The Federal Partners in Transition (FPT) is a workgroup with representatives of several federal agencies, including the Department of Education, the Department of Health and Human Services, the Department of Labor, and the Social Security Administration, which are involved in promoting inclusive service delivery for transitioning youth with disabilities from school into postsecondary education, the workforce, and independent living. FPT's Strategic Planning Committee, which comprises career and senior executive staff from the four aforementioned federal agencies, developed this interagency strategy to ensure our federal programs and resources are optimized to support our nation's youth and young adults with disabilities in reaching their goals of economic empowerment and independence. The partner agencies wish to acknowledge the national online dialogue participants and political and career staff for their input, dedication, and leadership throughout this process.

PARTICIPATING DEPARTMENTS AND AGENCIES

Department of Education

Office of Special Education and Rehabilitative Services (OSERS)[1]

Office of Postsecondary Education (OPE)

Office of Career, Technical, and Adult Education (OCTAE)

Institute of Education Sciences (IES)

Department of Health and Human Services

Administration for Community Living (ACL)

Health Resources and Services Administration (HRSA)

Assistant Secretary for Planning and Evaluation (ASPE)

Substance Abuse and Mental Health Services Administration (SAMHSA)

National Institutes of Health (NIH)

Centers for Medicare & Medicaid Services (CMS)

Administration for Children and Families (ACF)

Centers for Disease Control and Prevention (CDC)

Department of Labor

Employment and Training Administration (ETA)

Office of Disability Employment Policy (ODEP)

Wage and Hour Division (WHD)

Social Security Administration

Office of Research, Demonstration, and Employment Supports (ORDES)

The 2020 Federal Youth Transition Plan: A Federal Interagency Strategy was prepared by the Federal Partners in Transition (FPT) Workgroup. This report is reflective of FPT's multifaceted, cross-systems approach to provide supports and services to youth with disabilities and does not necessarily reflect the policies and legislative requirements of individual federal departments and agencies.

---

1 The Workforce Innovation and Opportunity Act (WIOA) reauthorizes programs previously authorized under the Workforce Investment Act of 1998, including programs under the Rehabilitation Act of 1973. The new statutory provisions incorporate "independent living" into the name and mission of NIDRR (National Institute on Disability, Independent Living and Rehabilitation Research) and move the program's administration from the Department of Education to the Administration on Community Living in the Department of Health and Human Services. In this document, the program name, NIDRR, is used to be consistent with the time period during which the 2020 Plan was developed.

TABLE OF CONTENTS

[Page Left Intentionally Blank]

PREFACE

An Inclusive Approach to Improving Transition Outcomes for Youth with Disabilities

To move toward national policies that will, by extension, lead to better outcomes for youth with disabilities[2] and others, the Federal Partners in Transition (FPT) Workgroup aims to embed equality, diversity, inclusion, and opportunity into its policy work. Doing so ensures our federal interagency strategy "removes disability from the special shelf" and reflects the underlying spirit of civil rights laws like the Individuals with Disabilities Education Act (IDEA), the Rehabilitation Act of 1973 (Rehabilitation Act), as amended by the Workforce Innovation and Opportunity Act 2014 (WIOA), and the Americans with Disabilities Act (ADA), which promote the full inclusion, integration, and participation of youth and adults with disabilities. Transition provisions recently enacted by WIOA are consistent with the principles, goals and policy priorities identified in *The 2020 Federal Youth Transition Plan: A Federal Interagency Strategy (2020 Plan)*.

To move towards an inclusive approach to transition outcomes for youth with disabilities, it is important to understand the challenges this population faces, the various systems they can access for services and supports, and their experience in the wider context of youth transition. An abundance of data exists describing the challenges youth with disabilities confront as they prepare for adult life, but there is also significant variation in the consistency of the data used to estimate the total size of this population. In part, this fluctuation stems from the varying ways disability is defined across the public programs and statistical agencies that collect these data. In 2012, Mathematica researchers Todd Honeycutt and Dave Wittenburg determined that the prevalence of disability ranges anywhere from 5 percent to nearly 14 percent of the total population of transition-age youth depending on the definitions and data sources used. Because of challenges inherent in quantifying the population of transition-age youth with disabilities and the fact that youth with disabilities are an inherent part of other specific youth populations such as "vulnerable" and "disconnected" youth, youth policy analysts and researchers have suggested developing a single overarching federal policy that addresses the challenges faced by youth in transition (Fernandes, 2012; Moreno, Honeycutt, McLeod, & Gill, 2013).

Understanding how multiple spheres of influence impact transition outcomes for youth with disabilities, FPT bases its strategy on the fact that youth with disabilities receive supports and services from child and adult service systems. In addition, they receive supports and services from mainstream systems as well as disability-focused systems. For instance, today 48 percent of students with disabilities who are served under IDEA are instructed in general education classrooms for at least 80 percent of the day. Thus, general education teachers are increasingly responsible for educating students with disabilities (West, 2009). The National Longitudinal Transition Study-2 (NLTS2)[3] collected data from parents and youth regarding postsecondary education for youth, ages 17 - 21, who had exited high school. The data indicated that 55 percent of postsecondary students who were identified by their secondary schools as having a disability did not consider themselves to have a disability by the time they transitioned to postsecondary school. The NLTS2 also reported that 37 percent of postsecondary students with disabilities identified themselves as having a disability and informed their postsecondary schools of their disability. Additionally, data reported to the Department of Education (ED) indicate that of the 392,200 students with disabilities, ages 14 - 21, in the United States, outlying areas, and freely associated states, who left school during the

The National Longitudinal Transition Study-2 (NLTS2), commissioned by the U.S. Department of Education, is a 10-year-long study of the characteristics, experiences, and outcomes of a nationally representative sample of youth with disabilities. It includes 11,270 youth nationwide who were ages 13 through 16 at the start of the study (2000). Information was collected over 10 years from parents, youth, and schools and it provided a national picture of the experiences and achievements of young people as they transition into early adulthood.

---

2 Youth with disabilities is defined differently by various programs and systems, including agencies contributing to *The 2020 Federal Youth Transition Plan: A Federal Interagency Strategy*. Consequently, a standard definition is not used in this report.
3 The NLTS2 is available at: http://nlts2.org/index.html.

2011- 2012 school year, 250,672 (63.9 percent) exited high school with a regular high school diploma, and 80,469 (20.5 percent) dropped out of school. The remaining 61,059 (15.6 percent) of students with disabilities, ages 14 - 21, who left school during the 2011 - 2012 school year, were reported as having received a certificate, reached maximum age, or died (Department of Education, 2012).[4]

Regarding employment, the NLTS2 reports in 2005, 57 percent of out-of-high-school students with disabilities were employed compared to 66 percent of students in the general population. Young adults with disabilities earned an average of $10.40 per hour compared with $11.40 per hour for young adults in the general population. Although employment outcomes for transition-age youth with disabilities have improved over the past decade, youth with disabilities continue to lag behind their peers without disabilities in finding a job. In May 2014, the employment rate for youth with disabilities, ages 16 to 19, was 15.1 percent, as compared to 27.3 percent for their peers without disabilities. The employment rate for youth with disabilities, ages 20 to 24, was 30.2 percent, and 63.9 percent for youth without disabilities (Bureau of Labor Statistics, 2014). In addition to low employment rates, youth with disabilities frequently rely on public benefits. For example, in 2012, 1.15 million youth (ages 13 to 25) received Supplemental Security Income (SSI) benefits, and another 167,000 youth (age 25 and under) received Social Security Disability Insurance (SSDI) benefits (Social Security Administration, 2012).

Furthermore, up to 75 percent of youth with disabilities have hidden or non-apparent disabilities, including mental health needs. Hidden disabilities are not readily apparent through observation; in addition, some disabilities emerge in young adulthood and may not yet be recognized or acknowledged by an individual or his or her parents. Therefore, to ensure young people with disabilities receive continuity of service and are connected to the range of transition services and supports they need, ED, Department of Health and Human Services, Department of Labor, and Social Security Administration are working together, within the parameters of their legislative authority, to ensure that all programs that serve youth - whether they are disability, mainstream, adult and/or child systems and programs - can be coordinated at the level of the individual intervention so that each person's needs are met as completely as possible.

Research also shows that larger social system factors should be taken into account when planning interventions because macrosystemic realities such as poverty, language, culture, and community unemployment can prevent diverse youth with disabilities from accessing opportunities (Trainor et al., 2008). Therefore, FPT is committed to promoting inclusive, comprehensive policies that ensure all youth with disabilities have access to the full range of both disability-related and general supports needed to reach their goals of economic empowerment and independence. For these reasons, FPT is committed to partnering with experts across multiple federal agencies and their respective programs to ensure that youth policies, programs, and services consider how multiple influences such as disability status, economic status, and sociocultural status impact youth in transition.

---

4 Consistent with 20 U.S.C. § 1418(a), States report data in what is known as the "618 data collection" using the ED*Facts* data system. One data element is "IDEA – Exiting Special Education," under which States report the number and percentage of children with disabilities by race, ethnicity, limited English proficiency status, gender, and disability category, who, for each year of age from age 14 through 21, stopped receiving special education and related services because of program completion (including graduation with a regular secondary school diploma), or other reasons, and the reasons why those children stopped receiving special education and related services. 20 U.S.C. § 1418(a) (1) (A)(iv).

EXECUTIVE SUMMARY

The FPT was formed in 2005 to improve interagency policy and service coordination to support all youth, including youth with disabilities, in successfully transitioning from school to adulthood. FPT brings together political, senior executive, and career staff from federal agencies across multiple systems to collaborate on transition issues. Several agencies' missions limit them to serving youth with disabilities, while others provide general youth services or a combination of disability-related and general services. The partnership is led by co-chairs, Kathy Martinez, Assistant Secretary for the Office of Disability Employment Policy at the Department of Labor (DOL), and Michael K. Yudin, Acting Assistant Secretary for the Office of Special Education and Rehabilitative Services at the Department of Education (ED). In February 2013, FPT formed a Strategic Planning Committee comprising career and senior executive staff from the ED, Department of Health and Human Services (HHS), DOL, and the Social Security Administration (SSA) to develop *The 2020 Federal Youth Transition Plan: A Federal Interagency Strategy (2020 Plan)* to improve transition outcomes for youth with disabilities. The 2020 Plan outlines how FPT will enhance interagency coordination through the identification of compatible outcome goals and policy priorities, ultimately leading to improved outcomes for youth with disabilities by 2020. The 2020 Plan was developed in response to the following recommendation from the Government Accountability Office (GAO):

"To improve the provision of transition services to students with disabilities through enhanced coordination among the multiple federal programs that support this population, we recommend that the Secretaries of Education, HHS, and Labor, and the Commissioner of SSA direct the appropriate program offices to work collaboratively to develop a federal interagency transition strategy." (GAO, 2012)

Specifically, GAO recommended that the strategy address: 1) compatible policies, procedures, and other means to operate across agency boundaries towards common outcomes for transitioning youth and their families; 2) methods to increase awareness among students, families, high school teachers, and other service providers on the range of available services; and 3) ways to assess the effectiveness of federal coordination efforts in providing transition services.

To develop a federal interagency strategy that works "across agency boundaries toward common outcomes" as recommended by GAO, FPT adopted the following shared vision.

Our vision is that all youth programs are based on universal design principles[5] so that youth, regardless of their individual challenges, including disability, are equipped to pursue a self-directed pathway to address their interests, aspirations, and goals across all transition domains including community engagement, education, employment, health, and independent living that will ultimately result in positive, everyday social inclusion.

Consistent with GAO's recommendation to improve the provision of transition services through enhanced coordination and compatible policies among the multiple federal programs that support transitioning youth with disabilities and their families, and using the shared vision as our guide, FPT also identified five compatible outcome goals. These five goals operate across agency boundaries and will underpin the overall federal interagency strategy moving forward.

---

5 Universal design is defined as the design of products and environments to be usable by all people, to the greatest extent possible, without the need for adaptation or specialized design. Retrieved from http://www.ncwd-youth.info/taxonomy/term/837.

To support positive outcomes for youth with disabilities, FPT is committed to partnering with experts across multiple federal agencies and their respective programs, including both disability and mainstream programs, to ensure that they are universally designed and accessible. As a result, youth with disabilities and all youth will have an equal opportunity to:

- **Access health care services and integrated work-based experiences in high school** to better understand how to manage their physical, mental, and emotional well-being, to enhance their job-readiness skills and career planning, and to make a successful transition from school to work and greater independence;

- **Develop self-determination and engage in self-directed individualized planning** to prepare them for postsecondary education, health care management, vocational training, and/or employment;

- **Be connected to programs, services, activities, information, and supports** for which they are eligible that prepare them to self-manage their health and wellness, pursue meaningful careers, become financially literate and capable, and make informed choices about their lives;

- **Develop leadership and advocacy skills** needed to exercise informed decision-making and personal and community leadership; and

- **Have involvement from families and other caring adults with high expectations** to support them in achieving their goals.

Additionally, the 2020 Plan highlights FPT's shared vision and current federal cross-systems initiatives that align with compatible outcome goals, as well as policy priorities that will inform FPT's work going forward. The FPT timeline for achieving the five compatible outcome goals is 2020.

INTRODUCTION: THE 2020 FEDERAL YOUTH TRANSITION PLAN, A FEDERAL INTERAGENCY STRATEGY

"We found interagency coordination is enhanced by having a clear and compelling rationale for staff to work across agency lines and articulate the common federal outcomes they are seeking." (GAO, 2012)

The purpose of the *2020 Federal Youth Transition Plan: A Federal Interagency Strategy* (2020 Plan) is to enhance interagency coordination, to develop compatible goals to improve outcomes for youth with disabilities in transition, and to help agencies approach transition in a more integrated way that will lead to improved outcomes by 2020. The 2020 Plan is intended to be the blueprint for the Federal Partners in Transition (FPT) Workgroup to carry out its efforts in response to the following recommendation from the Government Accountability Office (GAO) for executive action:

"To improve the provision of transition services to students with disabilities through enhanced coordination among the multiple federal programs that support this population, the Secretaries of Education, HHS, and Labor, and the Commissioner of SSA should direct the appropriate program offices to work collaboratively to develop a federal interagency transition strategy. This strategy should address: 1. compatible policies, procedures, and other means to operate across agency boundaries towards common outcomes for transitioning youth and their families; 2. methods to increase awareness among students, families, high school teachers, and other service providers on the range of available transition services; and 3. ways to assess the effectiveness of federal coordination efforts in providing transition services. To the extent that legislative changes are needed to facilitate the implementation of this transition strategy, agencies should identify and communicate them to the Congress."

The 2020 Plan consists of five additional sections. The first is a **Background** section, which includes a working definition of the term *transition* for the purposes of the 2020 Plan, describes the history of FPT, and discusses the assumptions that form an underlying foundation in carrying out our work. The second is a **Vision and Compatible Outcome Goals** section, which communicates FPT's shared vision, vision themes, and compatible outcome goals used to frame coordination across our federal agencies and respective programs. The third is an **FPT Approach** section, which discusses the positive impact of cross-systems coordination on youth's outcomes and describes the mixed methodology FPT employed in conducting its work. This work involved obtaining public input; obtaining information from agency experts; examining agencies' policies, procedures, and programs; and collaborating to share cross-systems expertise and establishing subgroups. The fourth is a **Federal Interagency Strategy in Action** section, which provides examples of current federal cross-systems initiatives that support the FPT compatible outcome goals. The fifth and final section is a **Policy Areas for Future Strategic Focus** section, which highlights the policy priorities that will inform FPT's work going forward.

BACKGROUND

What is transition?

The transition from youth to adulthood is critical for every young person. This is particularly true for young people with disabilities. Ideally, during the transition years, youth acquire knowledge and learn important skills they will need to maximize their independence and self-sufficiency in their communities. This process involves multiple domains including community engagement, education, employment, health, and independent living. It includes accessing educational opportunities including vocational training, obtaining employment, finding stable housing, and accessing health care and other resources to support their future planning and development into adulthood. Comprehensive access to these supports often requires that youth have accurate information and that strong cross-agency collaboration exists among youth service delivery systems, among adult service delivery systems, and between youth and adult service delivery systems. Without these networks and resources, individual youth, particularly those with disabilities, are at risk for poorer outcomes as they transition into adulthood.

What is transition? Transition is the period of time when adolescents are moving into adulthood and are often concerned with planning for postsecondary education, careers, health care, financial benefits, housing, and more. Research shows that regardless of eligibility and access challenges, there is a need to provide continuity of service for youth from ages 14 or 16 to ages 25 or 30 across child - and adult - service systems (Altschuler, 2005; Davis, n.d.; Davis & Sondheimer, 2005; Hoffman, Heflinger, Athay, & Davis, 2009; Manteuffel, Stephens, Sondheimer, & Fisher, 2008; Stewart et al., 2010).

Federal Partners in Transition Workgroup

First formed in 2005 to improve interagency coordination across the disability-related and general service systems, FPT convenes political, senior executive, and career staff from federal agencies including but not limited to ED, HHS, DOL, SSA, Corporation for National and Community Service (CNCS), and Department of Transportation (DOT). The partnership is led by co-chairs Kathy Martinez, Assistant Secretary for the Office of Disability Employment Policy at DOL, and Michael K. Yudin, Acting Assistant Secretary for the Office of Special Education and Rehabilitative Services at ED. By improving our understanding of each other's missions, research areas, policies, program practices, and research-based and evidence-based practices, FPT members are collaborating to develop processes, strategies, and solutions to support youth with disabilities, in creating an informed, self-directed pathway across all transition domains - as students, workers, parents, and community members.

Assumptions

The FPT interagency strategy is based on the following two assumptions:

- Each of the federal agencies and their respective programs contribute to positive transition outcomes in different ways within the context of their own unique programs' missions and statutory mandates. Although the agencies differ in terms of approach and terminology, targeted populations, and even the "way of doing business," much of the work is in fact complementary.

- Each agency, within the bounds of statutory authority, will continue to collaborate, coordinate, and contribute collectively to meeting the compatible outcome goals; and is committed and accountable to meet one or more goals. Most of these goals apply across youth transition programs and policies, regardless of systems.

VISION AND COMPATIBLE OUTCOME GOALS

To respond to GAO's recommendation, the strategic planning committee identified both a shared vision and a set of compatible outcome goals that will help guide future work by aligning programs and policies.

Vision

As the first step in developing a federal interagency strategy that works across agency boundaries and toward a common outcome, FPT adopted the following shared vision, which communicates the overarching desire for what FPT partners want for all youth transitioning to adulthood.

> *Our vision is that all youth programs are based on universal design principles so that youth, regardless of their individual challenges, including disability, are equipped to pursue a self-directed pathway to address their interests, aspirations, and goals across all transition domains including community engagement, education, employment, health, and independent living that will ultimately result in positive, everyday social inclusion.*

This federal interagency strategy focuses on the role of the federal government and FPT. Realizing this vision will require strong partnerships with other federal interagency workgroups, with state, local, tribal, and private sectors, as well as with youth with disabilities and their families as was stated in the Interagency Working Group on Youth Program's 2013 report, entitled *Pathways for Youth: Draft Strategic Plan for Federal Collaboration.*[6]

Vision Themes

To the extent that individual agencies have the capacity and flexibility to do so within existing statutory and resource constraints, FPT has identified the following themes to influence policy development, inform strategic direction, and drive long-term goals related to transition outcomes moving forward.

- **Begin with the end user in mind** - Youth with disabilities and their families are the primary stakeholders. They can affect or be affected by federally funded programs and policies. Therefore, youth and their families must be engaged in all stages of program and policy development.

- **Strength-based research, policies, and practices** - Transition services should be grounded in research-based and evidence-based practices that are inclusive, accessible, and strength-based to improve individual experiences for youth who have been historically underrepresented and economically disadvantaged. This includes youth who may be culturally and linguistically diverse, as well as LGBT youth. Given that additional research is foundational to making improvements across the systems and services, there is a need for continued national research studies to examine models that work and outcomes that matter.

- **Universal Design for Learning**[7] - Environments, products, and communication as well as programs, services, and activities designed with an inclusive spirit and universal design for learning structure are fundamentally beneficial for all youth and adult programs, and thus, for all individuals regardless of disability status. It is important to note, however, that certain entitlement programs for youth with disabilities are means-tested, have other strict disability-related requirements, and are intended by law to serve a targeted group of individuals.

- **Set high expectations** - Encourage self-determination and begin transition planning for youth with disabilities as early as possible to support a self-directed pathway to achieve optimal health and wellness, academic achievements, career goals and occupational planning, integrated employment, community inclusion, and independent living.

- **Options to live successfully in the community** - Youth with disabilities will not need to choose between work and health care supports to live successfully in the community.

---

6 The Pathways for Youth: Draft Strategic Plan for Federal Collaboration report is available at: http://www.findyouthinfo.gov/pathways-for-youth.
7 Universal Design for Learning (UDL) is defined as a framework for designing educational environments that help all students gain knowledge, skills, and enthusiasm for learning. Retrieved from http://www.ncwd-youth.info/taxonomy/term/839.

- **Person-centered planning** - Transition planning should be self-directed and strength-based with youth taking on increasingly greater decision-making and leadership roles as they move towards adulthood.

- **High-quality professional development for youth service professionals** - Youth service professionals must have access to high-quality professional development opportunities to ensure that they acquire the required competencies to effectively serve youth with disabilities.

- **Continuity of service and access to information** - The transition process is multifaceted. No one person, institution, or organization acting alone can provide all the supports and services needed. Therefore, FPT acknowledges that collaboration and coordination across systems, both disability-related and general, are imperative in providing continuity of service and access to information for youth and young adults.

FPT Compatible Outcome Goals for Transition Programs and Policies

To respond to GAO's recommendation to develop a coordinated federal interagency strategy, FPT initially conducted resource mapping to identify existing policies, programs, and outcome measures related to transition. We agreed that our approach to the mapping should be inclusive, recognizing that any federal program with a stated goal to serve all youth should be accessible to those with disabilities. For example, a program designed to prevent all teen pregnancy should be universally designed to ensure that young people with disabilities benefit from it. We mapped from the position that youth with disabilities are, first and foremost, youth, and that all youth programs and services should be both available to, and inclusive of, youth with disabilities. Preliminary review of these policies, program practices, and outcome measures generated the shared vision statement that expresses our hope for universal design principles to be applied to all youth programs in the future. Using the vision statement as a springboard, we then developed the following five compatible outcome goals that will operate across agency boundaries to improve transition outcomes for all youth with disabilities.

These compatible outcome goals reflect our belief that federal programs serving all youth transitioning to adult life should be universally designed and accessible in order to ensure that youth with disabilities and others have the equal opportunity to:

- **Access health care services and integrated work-based experiences in high school** to better understand how to manage their physical, mental, and emotional well-being, and to enhance their job-readiness skills and career planning. Research shows that having a competitive paid job during secondary school is the strongest predictor of job success after graduation (Colley and Jamison, 1998; Luecking and Fabian, 2000; Wagner et al. 2005). Furthermore, according to the 2011 - 2012 National Survey of Children's Health, 25.1 percent of children ages 12-17 have special health care needs (McManus et al, 2013). Youth with disabilities have been shown to have greater medical needs than their peers without disabilities and depend on a range of health care services for normal functioning and healthy development (Newacheck & Kim 2005; White, 2002; Zwerling, Whitten, & Sprince, 2002).

- **Develop self-determination and engage in self-directed individualized planning** to prepare youth with disabilities for postsecondary education, health care management, vocational training, and/or employment. Research shows that such transition plans should be built from a comprehensive strength-based assessment that identifies the youth's skills and developmental levels, goals, and future objectives (Hagner, Malloy, Mazzone, & Cormier, 2008; Podmostko, 2007; Walters, et al. 2011). By gradually shifting responsibility for health-related tasks at a developmentally appropriate time, youth gain the knowledge, skills, and experience necessary to independently navigate the adult health care system successfully. The services provided should be "flexible, supportive, and customizable to individual needs" (Manteuffel, Stephens, Sondheimer & Fisher, 2008).

- **Be connected to programs, services, activities, information, and supports** for which they are eligible that prepare them to self-manage their health and wellness, pursue meaningful careers, become financially literate and capable, and make informed choices about their lives. This includes ensuring that existing mainstream youth transition programs integrate youth with disabilities in their services,

> FPT will continue to broaden local partnerships that provide youth with disabilities with transition supports such as schools, parent organizations, and employment networks, by working with communities.

activities, information, and supports. Research shows that collaboration across systems serving youth with disabilities is an identified need (Osgood et al., 2010). For instance, studies show that when individuals receive support by multiple systems such as employment, transportation, and housing this will have direct and indirect impact on their health and access to care (Bean, 2013, Lindsay, 2011).

- **Develop leadership and advocacy skills** needed to exercise informed decision-making and personal and community leadership. These opportunities are key in transferring decision-making power to youth. Research shows that peer-to-peer mentoring and promoting youth leadership can help support youth move toward employment (Podmostko, 2007).

- **Have involvement from families and other caring adults with high expectations** to support them in achieving these goals. To achieve this, FPT will partner with families and other adults to ensure they have the information and supports they need to access appropriate services for youth in planning their future.

Research shows that youth with disabilities and their families need supports to help them navigate services available, both within each system and across the systems (Heflinger & Hoffman, 2008; Podmostko, 2007; Stewart et al., 2010). In a qualitative study of youth with disabilities involved in the U.S. Social Security Administration's Youth in Transition Demonstration, one-on-one relationships with counselors were vital to maintaining youth's drive to find work and to navigate "the system" (O'Day, 2012). Furthermore, family involvement can help promote positive school outcomes by helping to build strengths in youth with disabilities as they access employment information and assistance in accessing additional supports (Podmostko, 2007).

> Becoming financially literate and capable is not only desirable; it is often a way out of poverty. Counseling is vital when educating youth and their families about how work impacts benefits and how supports can continue while youth and young adults with disabilities transition to financial independence.

The Case for Collaboration

Given the complex needs of youth with disabilities and their families, policymakers and other professionals have stressed the importance of adopting broad-based partnerships across both disability-related and general systems that serve youth and young adults to ensure that youth in transition have access to a comprehensive set of services and supports to help them develop the skills they will need to manage their life, health and wellness; graduate from high school; access postsecondary education; and secure meaningful employment at a family-sustaining wage with pathways to career advancement. Second, it has also become evident that cross-agency strategies and practices are needed for performance design planning; collecting and using data; performance accountability; and the implementation of programs and services at the federal, state, and local levels. FPT understands that no single system or agency is responsible for providing all the necessary supports to help youth develop those skills; rather, as youth move from the classroom into the workplace, they often need to access services from several different agencies at one time in order to have their needs met. Therefore, FPT recognizes that cross-agency coordination and collaboration are needed both within and across child-and adult-service systems in order to effectively meet the diverse and complex needs of transitioning youth with disabilities.

FPT APPROACH

How FPT Fosters Collaboration

To carry out a federal interagency strategy, FPT is using a multistep approach. Figure I below highlights the strategies used.

Figure I. FPT Approach

Identification of legislative barriers to effectively implement transition services	Description of methods and strategies to develop compatible outcome goals for transition programs	Identification of strategies and tools to develop and use a single system for assessment of the effectiveness of transition programs	Review of strategies for each agency to share pertinent data across programs
Obtaining Public Input and Gathering Supporting Documentation (i.e., national online dialogue)	Examining Agencies' Policies, Procedures, and Programs (i.e., agencies' program goals and youth transition frameworks)	Collaborating to Share Administrative, Research, Evaluation, and Program Data	

Obtaining Public Input

To address GAO's point regarding statutory and regulatory barriers and to achieve the Administration's commitment to "creating an unprecedented level of openness in government," in May 2013, FPT hosted a two-week, national online dialogue, "Join the Conversation for Change: Help shape federal agency strategies for helping youth and young adults with disabilities successfully transition from school to work." Policymakers, service providers, advocates, youth, and others were invited to examine the impact of existing federal regulations and legislation on the successful transition from school to work of youth with disabilities. During the two-week dialogue, more than 3,000 participants contributed 355 ideas, more than 1,600 comments, and close to 10,000 votes. Visitors were given an opportunity to "vote" for ideas, which helped organize public input to determine possible solutions to ensure that youth with disabilities benefit from federal resources to realize their goals of economic empowerment and maximum independence. The results of the dialogue, which informed the FPT's compatible outcome goals as well as the policy priorities the agencies have identified in this report will continue to be a focal point for future activities. The *Federal Partners in Transition National Online Dialogue Participation Metrics Final Report*[8] outlines the results of the dialogue. Figure II below highlights the most popular ideas[9] the national online dialogue's participants provided for each campaign.

8　The Federal Partners in Transition National Online Dialogue Participation Metrics Final Report is available at: http://fptepolicyworks.ideascale.com/community-library/accounts/90/909643/FPT-National-Dialogue-Metrics-Report_September-2013-FINAL-a.pdf.

9　These direct quotes are from the national online dialogue.

Figure II. Most Popular Ideas Related to Statutory and Regulatory Barriers, and Solutions for Each Campaign

Campaigns	Most Popular Ideas
Education	**Lower Age for Starting Transition** "The age to begin transition service planning should be lowered back to 14, or sooner. Waiting to age 16 to initiate planning is too late."
Employment	**Make Adult Services Transferable Between States** "Currently, if a person who continues to need employment support is funded for that support in one state, parents are unable to leave that state without losing that support. A move can mean going to the end of a very long waiting list. IEPs[10] transfer from state to state. Adult services should, also."
Health and Human Services	**No Waiting for Services for Individuals with Disabilities** "Individuals with disabilities should not be on waiting lists for 8 years before they receive assistance. There should be a NO WAIT IN ANY STATE POLICY for services for individuals with disabilities."
Social Security	**Ability to Save for a Child** "As a parent, the responsible thing to do for my daughter is to save money in a college fund for her. However, because she is a minor, the account should legally be in my name. According to current SSI and Medicaid guidelines, I cannot have more than $1,500 between my checking and savings account so it is impossible for me to save money for her. Of course, I know there are ways around this but it should not be difficult for me to do the same thing an able-bodied parent can do at the drop of a hat."

Gathering Supporting Documentation

In addition to what we learned from the national online dialogue, FPT member agencies consulted with their internal experts to ensure that the lessons learned from current practice and the results of our respective research inform execution of this 2020 Plan. FPT also examined proposals that, if adopted, represent further opportunities to work collaboratively across our agencies, two examples of which are featured below:

- The Fiscal Year (FY) 2015 President's budget calls for $5 million in first-time funding under the Department of Health and Human Services' Administration on Community Living for a Youth Transitions Initiative. This funding would address the comprehensive needs of youth with intellectual and developmental disabilities as they transition from adolescence into young adult life across all systems - health, education, employment, human services, and community living. Federal, state, and local laws, regulations, and policies that contribute as barriers to employment for youth with intellectual and developmental disabilities (I/DD) will be identified and plans will be developed to deconstruct such barriers, and implement cross-agency programs to produce better outcomes for youth in transition.

- The FY 2015 President's Budget calls for the reauthorization of modified demonstration project authority under Section 234 of the Social Security Act for SSDI and conforming changes to SSI demonstration authority, in tandem with a detailed description of three potential early intervention pilots. This initiative would allow partnerships with other federal agencies in implementation, as appropriate.

---

10 IEPs *stand for Individualized Education Programs*

Examining Agencies' Policies, Procedures, and Programs - The First Step Towards Developing Compatible Outcome Goals

To address GAO's recommendation regarding development of compatible policies supporting common outcomes for transitioning youth and their families, FPT's strategic planning committee has worked closely with its partners both within and across the departments and agencies to examine agencies' policies, procedures, and programs through the use of resource-mapping activities. Having this basic knowledge about how the agencies operate in terms of eligibility requirements, program goals, allowable activities, and outcome measures is foundational to our ultimate goal of better aligning programs and policies to create a more seamless, coordinated transition system. To develop the compatible outcome goals mentioned in the **Vision and Compatible Outcome Goals** section, FPT relied on the knowledge base about what transition supports youth with disabilities need, keeping in mind that they are first and foremost youth and that all youth programs should be available to and inclusive of youth with disabilities. In addition, to provide organizational structure, FPT also examined a variety of the agencies' research-based and evidence-based youth transition frameworks in light of the following criteria to select a youth transition framework that: 1) had been adopted and implemented by federal partners across systems; 2) had been designed to ensure that all youth, including those with disabilities, receive a "continuum of service" across agency boundaries; and 3) included multiple transition domains, accounting for each agencies' program goals and statutory requirements.

Because the *Guideposts for Success*[11] (*Guideposts*) framework was used to gather information for ED's Office of Special Education and Rehabilitative Services' Promoting Readiness of Minors in Supplemental Security Income (PROMISE) initiative as well as to shape recent service delivery, policy, and technical assistance efforts related to other youth with disabilities initiatives (e.g., DOL's Disability Employment Initiative and SSA's Youth Transition Demonstration), FPT used the five elements from the *Guideposts* as an organizational framework to develop the compatible outcome goals. In so concluding, the strategic planning committee noted that there were commonalities that existed between the *Guideposts* and other youth transition frameworks.[12]

The *Guideposts* were designed based on the assumption that no single agency can meet all the transition needs of youth with disabilities, and that extensive collaborative partnerships are needed to ensure "continuum of service" across agency boundaries. Given their focus on achieving comprehensive service delivery by working across systems, the *Guideposts* provide an organizational framework through which we can demonstrate how our agencies' efforts and program goals are compatible, contribute to our shared vision for youth, and address the needs of youth with disabilities, many of which they have in common with other youth.

Collaborating to Share Administrative, Research, Evaluation and Program Data

To address GAO's recommendation regarding assessment of program effectiveness, in fall 2013, the National Collaborative on Workforce and Disability for Youth (NCWD/Youth), a National Technical Assistance and Demonstration Center on Preparing Youth with Disabilities for Employment funded by the Office of Disability Employment Policy (ODEP), conducted an extensive analysis of transition-related outcome measures and metrics and created a matrix of those sources, entitled the Crosswalk of Youth Progress and Outcome Measures for Transition. This work examined: 1) individual client progress and outcomes; 2) use of common definitions; 3) program design and systems improvement measures; and 4) professional development strategies across systems.

The overall goal of this work is to develop, in collaboration with our agency partners, their technical experts, and other experts in the field, a framework to improve transition-related data collection, data sharing, and use among providers, programs, systems, and policymakers at the local, state, and national levels, as well as with governmental

---

11 The *Guideposts for Success* framework, developed by the National Collaborative on Workforce and Disability for Youth (NCWD/Youth), in collaboration with the Office of Disability Employment Policy, reflects what research identifies as key educational and career development interventions that make a positive difference in the lives of all youth, including youth with disabilities including: (a) school-based preparatory experiences, (b) career preparation and work-based learning experiences, (c) youth development and leadership, (d) connecting activities, and (e) family engagement. The *Guideposts for Success* are available at: http://www.ncwd-youth.info/guideposts.

12 The National Secondary Transition Technical Assistance Center *Cross-referencing the Taxonomy for Transition Programming with NASET National Standards & Quality Indicators and Guideposts for Success for Transition-Age Youth* is available at: http://www.nsttac.org/sites/default/files/assets/pdf/pdf/capacity_building/CrosswalkTaxonomy.pdf.

and nongovernmental organizations across multiple systems. The information and measures ultimately gleaned through this effort will provide valuable information, which will assist the agencies in their decision-making regarding how best to assess the effectiveness of their transition-related programs and services, particularly discretionary ones, where the agencies have more flexibility.

Initial efforts related to data sharing focused on learning from our agency partners where such sharing is already occurring, and on barriers that might impede data sharing. One example of a federal data sharing agreement is the one between SSA and the Corporation for National and Community Service (CNCS) to determine to what extent CNCS impacts people in their programs, including youth with disabilities who are recipients of SSI and SSDI. No personally identifiable information is shared between CNCS and SSA. Another example is an agreement between ED and SSA which established procedures and conditions under which SSA and ED will continue to share aggregated information from certain SSA and ED databases. This information sharing will help agencies better address critical issues pertaining to individuals with disabilities, including the employment of youth and adults with disabilities.

GAO encouraged data sharing as a means to more effective interagency collaboration. For instance, GAO indicated that interagency working group members should identify and share relevant performance data in order to coordinate their efforts (GAO, 2014). In particular, data sharing enables agencies to extend their combined reach across systems and move beyond individual program-specific interventions. In addition, agencies could share "interoperable, open-source analytical tools and techniques" that streamline data collection and management efforts into a single system for use by multiple agencies (GAO, 2013).

However, the Government Data Sharing Community of Practice forum participants also raised immediate challenges to federal data sharing (GAO, 2014). For example, the lack of uniform data standards across agencies complicates the interaction of separate data sets. Moving to a standardized system could also prove costly to procure and implement even if the long-term cost-saving benefits are clear. In the case of delivering human services, GAO recommended several best practices from 35 stakeholders, including providing multiagency guidance on permissible data sharing and showcasing model data-sharing agreements in compliance with privacy regulations. Many proponents urge agencies to strike a balance through sharing enough systems and data to see the big picture without sacrificing government flexibility or individual agency missions. With regard to research data, agencies must qualify for a restricted use data license, establish a Memorandum of Agreement (MOA), limit the number of staff that can access the data, and follow strict security guidelines in order to obtain the use of restricted research data collected through large-scale federal surveys. Most of these steps are required to protect the personally identifiable information stored by the federal government, and all agencies understand the vital need to protect the personal data of those we serve. FPT plans to move forward on data sharing by fostering the collaboration necessary to promote effective and secure data sharing.

To further explore opportunities to share data across federal agencies and programs, FPT established a program and research data subgroup, comprising experts in program data and research data across different systems and fields. The program and research data subgroup will gather program- and research-related data information from across the partner agencies. To broaden the scope of this research and data collection effort, a Transition Research Inventory form was developed that captures youth-related data and research findings that are not directly connected to specific agency programs and offers supplemental research-based knowledge related to youth issues. Once this task is completed, the program and research subgroup will identify the opportunities and challenges associated with data sharing and carefully consider how and to what extent data collection between FPT partner agencies can and should be enhanced. Some of the questions the subgroup will continue to explore include:

- What are the challenges in supporting state and local programs in collaborating on the development of performance measurement systems?

- What benefits would result from this effort?

- What will it take to effectively support state and local entities to develop, implement, and use performance measurement systems in the improvement of programs and services?

- What are the essential components for achieving results?
    - For all youth and specific subpopulations, such as youth with disabilities, foster care youth, and juvenile justice youth?
    - Within and across systems?
- How can progress and outcome measures help improve interagency collaboration?

Each of these aforementioned strategies has provided FPT with insight on multiple levels and enhanced our knowledge and coordination across systems. The process led to continuous, candid dialogue among the partners and fostered a climate of cooperation and mutual benefit among the agencies. The preparation of this 2020 Plan and our other activities are designed to ultimately lead to improved interagency collaboration and, by extension, positive transition outcomes for youth with disabilities by 2020.

FEDERAL INTERAGENCY STRATEGY IN ACTION

Below are existing priorities, initiatives, and cross-agency activities that are aligned with our compatible outcome goals:

Administration on Intellectual and Developmental Disabilities' (AIDD) Partnerships in Employment Systems Change Grants

The AIDD Partnerships in Employment Systems Change Grants[13] are funded under Projects of National Significance. These eight grantees have partnered with state agencies, including the state Department of Education, State Vocational Rehabilitation (VR), State agency delivering Developmental Disabilities (DD) Medicaid Services, and the State DD Councils, to form a consortium that will develop and conduct initiatives designed to improve employment outcomes, expand competitive employment in integrated settings, and improve statewide system policies and practices for youth and young adults with intellectual and developmental disabilities (I/DD). In addition, a Community of Practice project serves additional states. The goal of the project is to build capacity, reform delivery systems, and improve strategies related to competitive integrated employment. This work leverages expertise from ODEP's Employment First Initiative and the State Employment Leadership Network, and is a partnership of the National Association of State Directors of Developmental Disability Services and the Institute for Community Inclusion at the University of Massachusetts Boston.

Disability Employment Initiative (DEI)

DEI[14] seeks to improve education, training, and employment opportunities and outcomes of youth and adults with disabilities who are unemployed, underemployed, and/or receiving Social Security disability benefits. The DEI is jointly funded and administered by DOL's Employment and Training Administration (ETA) and ODEP. DEI improves collaboration among employment and training and asset development programs implemented at state and local levels, including SSA's Ticket to Work Program, and builds effective partnerships that leverage resources to better serve individuals with disabilities. Because expanding the workforce investment system's capacity to serve as Employment Networks for SSA disability beneficiaries is a primary goal of the grant, DOL also works closely with SSA in implementing it. Since 2010, DOL has awarded over $81 million in grants to 26 states through the initiative. DEI Projects focus on either adults or youth in order to develop and refine replicable models. Youth-related DEI Projects must implement a service delivery strategy consistent with the *Guideposts*.

Employment First

ODEP investments in Employment First[15] have fostered strong interagency collaboration on a focused goal at the state and the federal level to promote integrated employment as the preferred outcome of day and employment services for individuals with the most significant disabilities. The Employment First State Leadership Mentoring Program (EFSLMP) is a cross-disability, cross-systems change initiative focused primarily on helping various publicly financed systems at the state level forge strong partnerships in supporting a common customer to achieve success in integrated employment through the alignment of policy, funding, and service delivery strategies. Participating states must commit to having, at a minimum, the following state agencies engaged in the EFSLMP: education, I/DD adult services, Medicaid, mental health, VR, and workforce investment. States typically have an independent division of I/DD services, or it is housed as a subdivision of a state's Medicaid agency or Department of Health and Human Services. ODEP has utilized the observations from working with 32 state teams to educate policymakers across the federal government, sharing information on existing federal public policies that either enhance or impede state Employment First systems-change efforts. These activities have helped inform the work of the Federal Interagency Community Employment Working Group, as well as helped inform the development of policy guidance and recommendations to the Centers for Medicare & Medicaid Services (CMS), ETA, and ED's Rehabilitation

---

13 Information on AIDD Partnerships in Employment Systems Change Grants is available at: http://www.acl.gov/Programs/AIDD/Programs/PNS/Resources/PartnershipsInEmplSystemsChangeGrants.aspx.

14 Information on DEI is available at: http://www.dol.gov/odep/topics/DEI.htm.

15 Information on Employment First is available at: http://www.dol.gov/odep/topics/EmploymentFirst.htm

Services Administration (RSA). In 2014, ODEP will be embarking on the development of a National Employment First Strategic Policy Framework, which will embed cross-systems approaches and strategies for ensuring a solid policy framework focused on optimizing improved, integrated employment outcomes for citizens with significant disabilities.

Leadership Education in Neurodevelopmental and Other Related Disabilities

The Health Resources and Services Administration's (HRSA's) Maternal and Child Health Bureau (MCHB) funds 43 Leadership Education in Neurodevelopmental and Related Disabilities (LENDs) training programs in 39 states to improve the health of infants, children, and adolescents who have, or are at risk for developing, neurodevelopmental and other related disabilities by preparing trainees from a wide array of professional disciplines to assume leadership roles and ensure high levels of interdisciplinary clinical competence and a culturally diverse workforce. Many LEND programs promote effective transition consultation for students in the health, education, and employment realms even though their core mission is to provide clinical interdisciplinary leadership training to health practitioners and families. The LENDs, in conjunction with AIDD-funded University Centers for Excellence in Developmental Disabilities (UCEDDs) participate in multi-agency efforts to work to improve the service system for youth and young adults with disabilities. An example of such efforts is the Partnerships for Employment project, funded by the Administration for Community Living, which is working with eight states to improve employment outcomes for youth and young adults with I/DD.

Another example of multi-agency collaboration is the Family-Centered Transition Project,[16] which has received funding from the National Institute on Disability and Rehabilitation Research (NIDRR) in ED's Office of Special Education and Rehabilitative Services. In 2013, the LENDs and UCEDDs, with the Association of University Centers on Disability (AUCD), produced a report entitled, A Collaborative Interagency, Interdisciplinary Approach to Transition from Adolescence to Adulthood,[17] to highlight the interagency and interdisciplinary approaches that will facilitate effective transition process for youth with disabilities from adolescence to young adulthood.

Medicaid & The Health Insurance Marketplaces

The Affordable Care Act greatly improves the access of young adults to health care insurance through Medicaid[18] expansion in a number of states and the extension of dependent eligibility to age 26 in private employer insurance plans. Moreover, for youth in transition, who may be just starting out with income above the level of Medicaid eligibility, the Health Insurance Marketplaces provide a key potential source of insurance coverage for this population. Coverage purchased through the Marketplaces no longer has any lifetime or annual caps on essential health benefits and preexisting conditions exclusions have been eliminated. Removing such obstacles to coverage is particularly important to young adults with disabilities. Plans sold through the Marketplaces must also offer a core set of benefits known as the essential health benefits including pediatric services, mental health services and habilitation and rehabilitation services, among others. Young adults in transition, either by themselves or with their families, can confidently purchase coverage through the Marketplaces and receive financial assistance knowing that they will be able to access the services they need, when they need them. There are ongoing initiatives to educate this population on these benefits and support their access to quality health care. At the same time, innovations in clinical care, education, policy, and research are needed.

Medicaid is a joint federal and state program that is partially funded by the federal government and administered by states. Through various programmatic authorities, it provides states with opportunities to promote employment and successful community living for youth in transition. In addition, states have opportunities to test innovative strategies and transform their long-term care systems through demonstration waivers or increased funding within Affordable Care Act provisions. States also have the opportunity to promote employment and successful community living through the Medicaid Buy-In program, which permits states to allow higher income limits or no

---

16 Information on The Family-Centered Transition Project is available at: http://iod.unh.edu/Projects/fctp/project_description.aspx.
17 A Collaborative Interagency, Interdisciplinary Approach to Transition from Adolescence to Adulthood Report is available at: http://www.aucd.org/docs/publications/transition2013_full_sm2.pdf.
18 Information on Medicaid is available at: http://www.medicaid.gov/.

income limits for working individuals with disabilities, including youth in transition with disabilities. Forty-six states currently have Medicaid Buy-In programs.

As noted earlier, Employment First's activities have created opportunities to promote health care transition planning as it relates to employment by asking participating states to include Medicaid agencies as one of the required partners and working closely with CMS, ETA, and RSA. Furthermore, given that the ability to manage one's health is critical to going to school, learning, and transitioning into employment, ODEP established an alliance with the HSC Foundation's Youth Transition Collaborative and HHS' MCHB funded Center for Health Care Transition Improvement in April 2014. Recognizing the opportunities to transform health care transition planning through the Affordable Care Act, the alliance aims to provide stakeholders with information, technical assistance, and access to resources that will help build the capacity of regional and national organizations to empower youth, young adults, and young veterans with disabilities or chronic health conditions to create a self-directed path to integrated employment and optimal health and well-being.

National Institute on Disability and Rehabilitation Research (NIDRR) Co-funded Research in Transition

NIDRR, in ED's Office of Special Education and Rehabilitative Services, and the Substance Abuse and Mental Health Services Administration, in HHS, co-fund research centers that identify, develop, and evaluate transition practices for youth and young adults with serious mental health conditions. More information is available on the grantees' websites:

Rehabilitation Research and Training Center at University of Massachusetts Medical School[19]

Rehabilitation Research and Training Center at Portland State University[20]

Promoting Readiness of Minors in Supplemental Security Income (PROMISE)

The PROMISE[21] program is an initiative of ED, HHS, DOL, and SSA. Under this competitive grant program, state agencies have partnered to develop and implement a model demonstration project that provides coordinated services and supports designed to improve the education and career outcomes of children with disabilities receiving SSI, including services and supports to their families. The six PROMISE projects, funded by ED and awarded in FY 2013, provide opportunities for states to be innovative in designing programs that meet the needs of child SSI recipients and their families and that will improve the life outcomes of individuals with disabilities. Figure III below highlights the PROMISE States and Programs.

Figure III. PROMISE States and Projects

State(s)	Projects
Arkansas	Arkansas PROMISE 2013
California	California PROMISE (CaPROMISE)
Consortium of States - Utah, South Dakota, North Dakota, Montana, Colorado, and Arizona	Achieving Success by Promoting Readiness for Education and Employment (ASPIRE)
Maryland	Maryland PROMISE Promoting the Employment Readiness of SSI Minors
New York	New York State PROMISE
Wisconsin	Wisconsin PROMISE

---

19 Information on Rehabilitation Research and Training Center at University of Massachusetts Medical School is available at: http://labs.umassmed.edu/transitionsRTC/#sthash.VsPe5vPr.dpbs.

20 Information on Rehabilitation Research and Training Center at Portland State University is available at: http://www.rtc.pdx.edu/index.php.

21 Information on the PROMISE program is available at: http://www2.ed.gov/about/inits/ed/promise/index.html.

Rehabilitation Services Administration (RSA) Special Demonstration Transition Projects

In FY 2007, federal funds were provided to improve upon state-level collaboration and state interagency coordination for students with disabilities under the authority of RSA's Special Demonstration Programs. The purpose of the Special Demonstration Transition Projects was to provide financial assistance to eligible entities to expand and improve the provision of VR services and related services for youth with disabilities. These grants supported projects that demonstrated the use of collaborative transition planning and service delivery to improve postsecondary education and employment outcomes of youth with disabilities. As noted in the chart below, six states were awarded grants. The grantees received final funding in FY 2011, continued to operate during FY 2012, and at the end of that year, RSA approved no-cost extensions for all of these grants, which allowed them to operate through September 2013. Oregon was given an additional no-cost extension and operated through September 2014. Grantees collected data under a task order funded by RSA. This data was reviewed and compiled for future reference and dissemination to researchers and service providers. In addition, data and outcomes from the Maryland project are now being analyzed for dissemination to researchers and service providers (e.g.,Luecking & Luecking, 2014). Figure IV below highlights RSA's Special Demonstration Transition Projects' states, programs, and contacts.

Figure IV. RSA Special Demonstration Transition Programs

State(s)	Program
South Carolina	**Youth Employment Services (YES)** Provided a multitiered program that combines three transition models: Transition Employability, Skills Workforce Apprenticeship Program, and High School/High Technology.
Pennsylvania	**PA Community on Transition** Achieved employment outcomes through a shared agenda by replicating evidence-based models such as Project Search and Postsecondary Innovative Transition Technology.
Oregon	**ACCESS: Accelerated Career Counseling and Employment Support Services** Analyzed the effectiveness of the interagency planning, implementation process, and effects of project.
Maryland	**Maryland Seamless Transition Collaborative** Implemented a model of transition services that is characterized by student self-determination, work experiences, paid inclusive employment prior to school exit, and resource links.
Ohio	**Promoting Rehabilitation and Educational Results through State, Regional, and Local Collaboration** Collaborated with Ohio Rehabilitation Services Commission and the Office for Exceptional Children to address difficulties in accessing transition services due to the lack of planning.
Massachusetts	**Transition Works: Innovative Strategies for Transitioning Youth with Disabilities from School to Work and Post-Secondary Outcomes** Vocational Rehabilitation Counselors partnered with local school districts to support youth with disabilities through innovative practices and strategies.

Office of Special Education Programs (OSEP) and Rehabilitation Services Administration (RSA)

The National Technical Assistance Center on Improving Transition to Postsecondary Education and Employment for Students with Disabilities was funded at $2.5 million. OSEP and RSA jointly funded this National Technical Assistance Center to assist State Educational Agencies, Local Educational Agencies, State VR agencies, and other VR service providers to implement evidence-based and promising practices and strategies to ensure that students with disabilities, including those with significant disabilities, graduate from high school with the knowledge, skills, and supports needed for success in postsecondary education and employment.

Youth Transition Demonstration

The Youth Transition Demonstration[22] was a random assignment research study conducted by SSA. Demonstration projects were designed to help youth with disabilities maximize their economic self-sufficiency as they transition from school to work. The projects emphasized collaboration among and between multiple service systems: including, for example, schools and state VR agencies. The evaluation design was based on the *Guideposts for Success framework*, developed by ODEP in collaboration with NCWD/Youth. Through this research, SSA is developing and evaluating strategies that increase employment outcomes and independence for youth with disabilities as they transition to adulthood and employment. This research generated empirical evidence on the impacts of SSI waivers and enhanced coordination of services for youth with disabilities

---

22 Information on Youth Transition Demonstration is available at: http://www.ssa.gov/disabilityresearch/youth.htm.

POLICY AREAS FOR FUTURE STRATEGIC FOCUS

Based on the issues identified from FPT's multistep approach, including the public input we received from the national online dialogue and an analysis of transition-related efforts and proposals of individual agencies, FPT has committed to focus on the following policy priorities in order to achieve our compatible outcome goals and improve transition outcomes for youth with disabilities:

- Promote the benefits of work-based learning as a part of education and workforce training.

- Facilitate access to quality health care and health care insurance. Individuals should not have to choose between health care and working.

- Support professional development for service professionals, such as educators, job coaches, and health care providers to build competencies in asset-based service delivery approaches.

- Bridge the service gap between youth and adult programs to encourage and expand opportunities for students and youth with disabilities up to age 24 (e.g., dual enrollment, internships, mentorships, apprenticeships, and postsecondary training options).

- Enhance states' capacity to create developmental opportunities for youth with disabilities during school and after school.

- Demonstrate the value of hiring youth and young adults with disabilities from both an employee's and employer's perspective.

- Create a benefits counseling model to promote the concept of self-determination and person-centered planning.

- Increase capacity for systems change work within states, which could be similar to Employment First's Community of Practice where states could come together to share ideas and strategies for adopting policies and practices that lead to positive outcomes for youth in transition.

- Improve education and outreach to the public regarding policy and practices governing transition service programs.

- Promote collaboration, coordination, and cooperation among youth and adult service systems, state education agencies, state VR and workforce development agencies, schools, and youth with disabilities and their families and leverage expertise and resources to assist students with disabilities in achieving their postsecondary education and career goals.

- Evaluate and implement the evidence-based strategies identified through PROMISE model demonstration projects that have proven effective in improving outcomes for child SSI recipients and their families.

- Align policy and regulation to encourage younger SSA disability beneficiaries to achieve eventual financial independence with the assistance of programs like the Ticket to Work.

FPT expects the actions taken to implement these policies will ultimately lead to improved outcomes for youth with disabilities by 2020.

CONCLUSION

FPT has worked diligently since 2012 to address GAO's recommendation to work collaboratively to develop a federal interagency transition strategy. We will continue to work together and engage all partners in candid dialogue, enhancement of our knowledge base, the leveraging of available resources, and, most importantly, in modeling the type of collaboration across federal systems that is necessary at the state and local levels to achieve meaningful results. FPT will remain vigilant in developing a coordinated federal interagency transition strategy, which supports youth and young adults with disabilities in achieving their goals of economic empowerment and independence.

APPENDIX

List of Acronyms

A

ACF	Administration for Children and Families (HHS)
ACL	Administration for Community Living (HHS)
ADA	Americans with Disabilities Act
AIDD	Administration on Intellectual and Developmental Disabilities (HHS)
ASPE	Assistant Secretary for Planning and Evaluation (HHS)

C

CDC	Centers for Disease Control and Prevention (HHS)
CMS	Centers for Medicare & Medicaid Services (HHS)
CNCS	Corporation for National and Community Service

D

DEI	Disability Employment Initiative
DOL	Department of Labor
DOT	Department of Transportation

E

ED	Department of Education
EFSLMP	Employment First State Leadership Mentoring Program
ETA	Employment and Training Administration (DOL)

F

FPT	Federal Partners in Transition
FY	Fiscal Year

G

GAO	Government Accountability Office

H

HHS	Department of Health and Human Services
HRSA	Health Resources and Services Administration (HHS)

I

I/DD	Intellectual and Developmental Disabilities
IDEA	Individuals with Disabilities Education Act
IEP	Individualized Education Program
IES	Institute of Education Sciences

L

LENDS	Leadership Education in Neurodevelopmental and Related Disabilities

M

MCHB	Maternal and Child Health Bureau (HHS)
MOA	Memorandum of Agreement

N

NCWD/ Youth	National Collaborative on Workforce and Disability for Youth
NIDRR	National Institute on Disability and Rehabilitation Research (ED)
NIH	National Institutes of Health (HHS)
NLTS2	National Longitudinal Transition Study-2

O

OCTAE	Office of Career, Technical, and Adult Education (ED)
ODEP	Office of Disability Employment Policy (DOL)
OPE	Office of Postsecondary Education (ED)
ORDES	Office of Research, Demonstration, and Employment Support (SSA)
OSERS	Office of Special Education and Rehabilitative Services (ED)

P

PROMISE	Promoting Readiness of Minors in Supplement Security Income

R

RSA	Rehabilitation Services Administration (ED)

S

SAMHS	A Substance Abuse and Mental Health Services Administration (HHS)
SSA	Social Security Administration
SSDI	Social Security Disability Insurance
SSI	Supplemental Security Income

U

UDL	Universal Design for Learning

W

WHD	Wage and Hour Division (DOL)

Y

YES	Youth Employment Services

REFERENCES

Altschuler, D. M. (2005). Policy and program perspectives on the transition to adulthood for adolescents in the juvenile justice system. In D.W. Osgood, E.M. Foster, C. Flanagan, & G.R. Ruth (Eds.) *On your own without a net: The transition to adulthood for vulnerable populations* (pp. 92-113). Chicago: University of Chicago Press.

Bean, K. F., Shafer, M. S., & Glennon, M. (2013). The impact of housing first and peer support on people who are medically vulnerable and homeless. *Psychiatric Rehabilitation Journal, 36*(1), 48.

Bureau of Labor Statistics. (2014) Labor Force Statistics from the Current Population Survey. Retrieved from http://www.bls.gov/cps/.

Colley and Jamison, 1998; Luecking and Fabian, 2000; Wagner et al. 2005 (as cited in Fraker, T., 2013, February). *The youth transition demonstration: Lifting employment barriers for youth with disabilities* (Issue Brief No. 13-01). Washington, DC. Mathematica Policy Research.

Davis, M. (n.d). *Transition to Adulthood. Presentation.*

Davis, M., & Sondheimer, D.L. (2005). Child mental health systems' effort to support youth in transition to adulthood. *Journal of Behavioral Health Services and Research, 32,* 27-42.

Department of Education. (2012). 2011-2012 *IDEA Part B Exiting.* Retrieved from https://explore.data.gov/Education/2011-2012-IDEA-Part-B-Exiting/7mdz-8ya4.

Fernandes, A. L. (2012). *Vulnerable youth: Background and policies.* Congressional Research Service, DIANE Publishing.

Government Accountability Office. (2013). *Highlights of a forum: Data analytics for oversight & law enforcement* (GAO 13-680SP).

Government Accountability Office. (2014). *Managing for results: implementation approaches used to enhance collaboration in interagency in interagency groups.* Washington, DC (GAO 14-220).

Government Accountability Office. (2012). *Students with disabilities: Better federal coordination could lessen challenges in the transition from high school.* Washington, DC. (GAO 12-594).

Hagner, D., Malloy, J. M., Mazzone, M. W., & Cormier, G. M. (2008). Youth with disabilities in the criminal justice system: Considerations for transition and rehabilitation planning. *Journal of Emotional and Behavioral Disorders, 16*(4), 240-247. doi:10.1177/1063426608316019.

Heflinger, C. A. & Hoffman, C. (2008). *Transition age youth in publicly funded systems: Identifying high-risk youth for policy planning and improved service delivery. Journal of Behavioral Health Services & Research, 35*(4), 390-401.

Hoffman, C., Heflinger, C. A., Athay, M. & Davis, M. (2009). Policy, funding, and sustainability: Issues and recommendations for promoting effective transition systems. In H.B. Clark & D.K. Unruh (Eds.) *Transition of youth and young adults with emotional or behavioral difficulties: An evidence-supported handbook.* Baltimore, MD: Brookes Publishing Co.

Honeycutt, T., Thompkins, A., Bardos, M., & Stern, S. (2013). *State differences in the Vocational Rehabilitation experiences of transition-age youth with disabilities* (No. 7873). Washington, DC: Mathematica Policy Research.

Lindsay S. "Employment status and work characteristics among adolescents with disabilities." *Disabil Rehabil* 2011; *33*(10): 843-54.

Luecking, D. M., & Luecking, R. G. (2013). Translating Research Into a Seamless Transition Model. *Career Development and Transition for Exceptional Individuals*, 2165143413508978.

Manteuffel, B., Stephens, R.L., Sondheimer, D.L., & Fisher, S.K. (2008). Characteristics, service experiences, and outcomes of transition-aged youth in systems of care: Policy implications. *Journal of Behavioral Health Services & Research. 35*(4):469–487. doi:10.0007/s11414-008-9130-6.

McManus MA, Pollack LR, Cooley WC, McAllister JW, Lotstein D, Strickland B, Mann MY. "Current status of transition preparation among youth with special needs in the United States." *Pediatrics*. 2013 Jun; *131*(6): 1090-7.

Moreno, L., Honeycutt, T., McLeod, S., & Gill, C. (2013). *Lessons for programs serving transition-age youth: A comparative analysis of the US and 10 other countries in the Organisation for Economic Co-Operation and Development (OECD)* (No. 7766). Washington, DC: Mathematica Policy Research.

Newacheck P, Kim S. A national profile of health care utilization and expenditures for children with special health care needs. Arch Pediatr Adolesc Med 2005; *159*:10-17.

O'Day, B. (2012). *Youth Perspectives on the Transition to Adulthood.* Presentation at the Future for Young Americans with Disabilities: Economic Success or Dependence?

Osgood, D., Foster, E., & Courtney, M. E. (2010). Vulnerable populations and the transition to adulthood. *Future of Children, 20*(1), 209-229.

Podmostko, M. (2007). Tunnels and cliffs: A guide for workforce development practitioners and policymakers   serving youth with mental health needs. Washington, DC: National Collaborative on Workforce & Disability for Youth. *Institute for Educational Leadership.*

Social Security Administration. (2012). Retrieved from http://www.socialsecurity.gov/policy/docs/statcomps/ssi_asr/2012/sect06.html#table35 and http://www.socialsecurity.gov/policy/docs/statcomps/di_asr/2012/sect01b.html#table4.

Stewart, D., Freeman, M., Law, M., Healy, H., Burke-Gaffney, J., Forhan, M., ... & Guenther, S. (2010). Transition to adulthood for youth with disabilities: Evidence from the literature. International Encyclopedia of Rehabilitation.

Trainor, A. A., Lindstrom, L., Simon-Burroughs, M., Martin, J. E., & Sorrells, A. M. (2008). From marginalized to maximized: Opportunities for diverse youths with disabilities: A position paper of the division on career development and transition. *Career Development for Exceptional Individuals, 31*(1), 56-64.

West, J. (2009). *Increasing Access to Higher Education for Students with Disabilities and Strengthening the Preparation of Professionals who Instruct Them: The Higher Education Opportunity Act of 2008. Advances in Learning and Behavioral Disabilities,22*, 189-225.

White, P. "Access to health care: health insurance considerations for young adults with special health care needs/disabilities." *Pediatrics*. 2002; 110-1328-1335).

Zwerling, C., Whitten, P.S., Sprince, N.L., Davis, C.S., Wallace, R.B., Blanck, P.D., & Heeringa, S.G. (2002). Workforce participation by persons with disabilities: The National Health Interview Survey Disability Supplement 1994 to 1995. Journal of Occupational and Environmental Medicine, *44*(4), 358-364.

[Page Left Intentionally Blank]

www.ingramcontent.com/pod-product-compliance
Lightning Source LLC
Chambersburg PA
CBHW080800290526
45790CB00008B/3534